Finding My Way

A Book Of Feelings

ISHITA NARAIN

ISBN 979-8-88772-965-7

Dear Reader

We're about to become close friends. The pages to come unfold pieces of me I hold close to my heart. Abysmal insecurities, blissful epiphanies, hushed traumas, and hopeful dreamscapes. Writing this book has been wildly therapeutic and has brought me immense joy. Thinking of you having it in your hands makes me want to explode with happiness. I beg you to messy these pages. Take a Sharpie, highlighter, or paintbrush to it. Dog-ear, underline, scribble, and doodle as you go.

– Ishita

Contents

Not the same

People tell me I'm not the same anymore.

That I'm a bore.

They expect more.

Wait and watch and one day I'll roar.

War with myself

I'm at a war with myself.
Putting my feelings on a shelf.
Not knowing what to do with myself.
I just want to go back to my old self.

Draining

It was draining.
Watching you gaining.
All the loving.
I had been wanting.

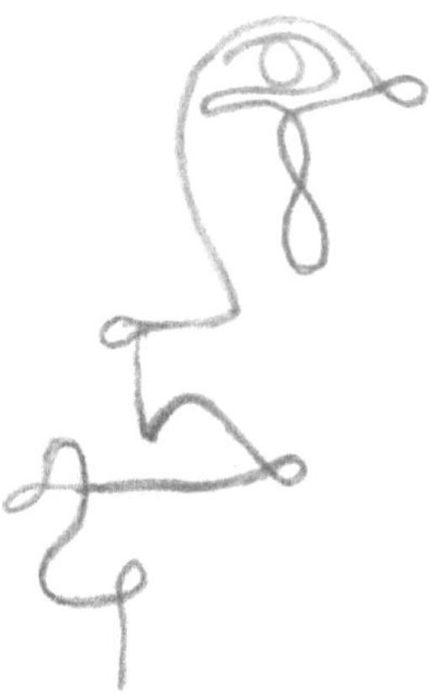

Said something that you didn't mean

You said you'd always be there.
As I looked for you everywhere.
But all I did was stare.
At the friendship that was never really there.

Criticise

I know how much you love to criticise.

You think you're very wise.

All you tell are lies.

As time just flies.

You left

We went from talking every night.
To our every conversation ending in a fight.
Wondering which one of us was right.
Guess we'll never know because you left right?

Enough

Spent time trying to be enough for you both.
Knew I'd never have any growth.
And now I loathe.
You both.

Lies

You tell me you're going to sleep.
How many lies can you keep?
The pain goes deep.
I can't do anything about it.
It stings a bit.
Your words hit.
Why can't you just admit?
That you never really cared for it.

Don't blame me

I'm out of sympathy.
So, please don't blame me.
Let me be.
What even were we?

You always lie

Looking up at the sky.
Wondering why
It was so hard to say goodbye
Even though you always lie.

Miss you

In some way.
I miss you every day.
Don't know what to say.
Just don't want this feeling to stay.

Never liked you

I never even liked you.

I know it's out of the blue.

I guess a part of me always knew.

I think you did too.

Bait

You used to be great.

Until I found out I was your bait.

It was probably fate.

And now all I experience is hate.

Haven't grown up at all

You haven't grown up at all.
Always managed to make me feel small.
You're so tall.
I had to build up a wall.

Despair

I was in despair.

Knew there was a lot to repair.

Forced myself to prepare.

But the situation was just so rare.

Existed

Don't get it twisted.
All the time I wasted.
Every problem you listed.
I wish you never existed.

Helpless

I was so helpless.
You couldn't care less.
Your problems were endless.
And why were you always so guiltless?

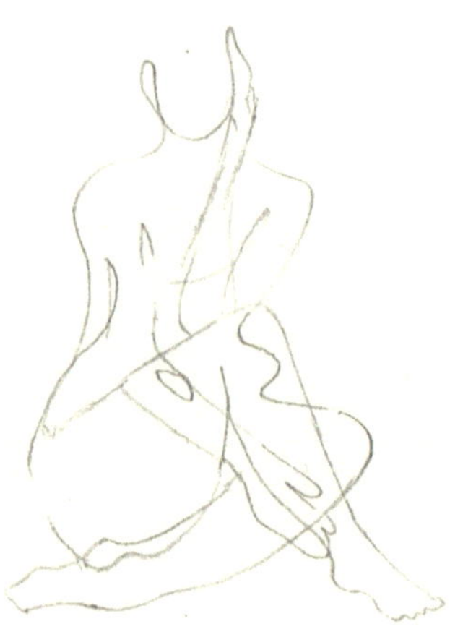

Wrong

I was wrong.
We got along.
But it wasn't for long.
But I was always strong.

Trusted

Asked you not to tell anyone.

But that's exactly what you had done.

I guess it was fun.

At that moment I was done.

Always

Why are you always so late?
All you do is talk about weight?
Why do you use the word hate?
Why do I always wait?

Ignore

You love to ignore.

I always wanted more.

But that was before.

You turned into a bore.

Wall

You never pick up my call.
You manage to make me feel small.
It's like you have built up a wall.
I always manage to fall.

Not the truth

I don't care.
But the truth is I really do.
I just can't bare.
The feeling of not getting through.

Preference

I was never the first preference.

All I needed was assurance.

You got me thinking I didn't have any importance.

Well now I have my independence.

Too late

I always asked if I could call.
I was ready to ignore all.
All you did was stall.
Never picking up my call.

Never wanted

I was never wanted.
You never responded.
I thought we bonded.
But now I'm just glad it ended.

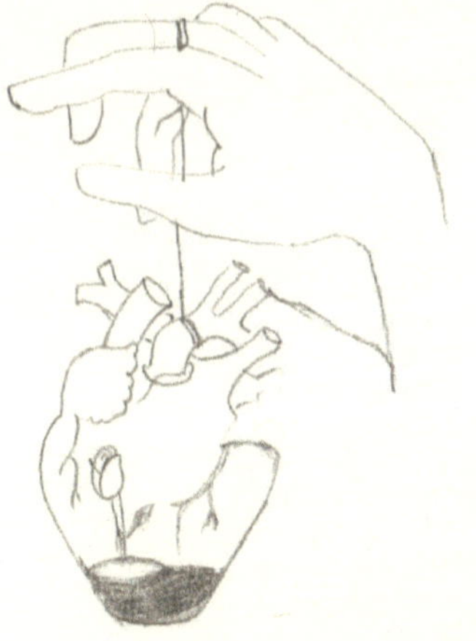

Care

Please don't tell me you care.

It isn't fair.

And I can't bare.

All this pain you have left me to spare.

Always comparing

Why do you compare?
I need some air.
What you did was unfair.
As I always waited for you to care.

Nothing lasts

Knew nothing could last.
Tried to forget about the past.
Your opinions were never asked.
Thank god I got out of it fast.

Fake

I stayed awake.
For your sake.
To take.
All the ache.
But you turned out to be fake.

Version

I miss the version of me I can't get back.

At least not for a while.

But I'll get there.

Despite what you have to say.

That day

I don't think I'll ever be able to forget about that day.
I wish there was a way.
What hurts is that you didn't have anything to say.
Knowing I cried the whole day.
I tried to keep my phone away.
But it's okay.
Because I did everything I possibly could.
To get through that day.

Jealously

Why are you always trying to prove that you're better
than me?
You always end up getting the sympathy.
You always end up hurting me
I guess it's just Jealousy.

Bored

I feel you both are getting bored of me.
I know you won't agree.
There's nothing you can guarantee.
And I'm really tired of the fake sympathy.

Talking to you

Talking to you was like poetry.
I knew it was going to end early.
You replied barely.
Handling it carelessly

Aftermath

I can't seem to deal with the aftermath of our friendship.
Now that you're gone.
I knew you were a thorn.
Always causing a storm.
I thought it was a phase.
But it went on.
Until I gave up.
And moved on.

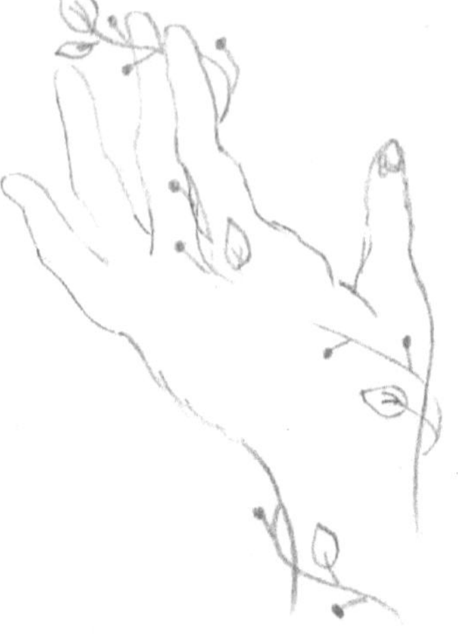

Boundaries

Who even picks up calls anymore
Maybe they're busy I think.
It hurts but I won't admit.
I wonder when I'll close that door.
I wonder when the pain will sink.
I wonder when I'll stop caring for it.

Freedom

I try not to think too much about your actions.
But I just can't help but think.
How you could be so happy?
Losing a friend that was worth the fight.
But who cares right?
It's all alright.
You gave up without a fight.

Wasted

The energy i invested in you.
Could've been invested in me.
I wish you remember that for the rest of your life.
It's a regret I'll always have.

Take a look

Why do you always correct people?
It's because you have nothing better to do.
I wonder why you don't look at yourself first.
Before looking for flaws in everyone else.

Ruined

To hear you say I've ruined everything else.

Made me question myself.

You made me believe I had no value.

And now I have made it a point to never listen to you.

And hear your wonderful opinions.

Because I learned to make my own decisions.

Always there

I was there.

All you had to do was care.

I just couldn't bare.

Knowing there was still a lot to repair.

Tears

I laughed through tears.
When I finally faced my fears.
After all these years.
I heard cheers.

The day I was born

The day I was born.
A beautiful sun was drawn.
It was warm.
In my final form.

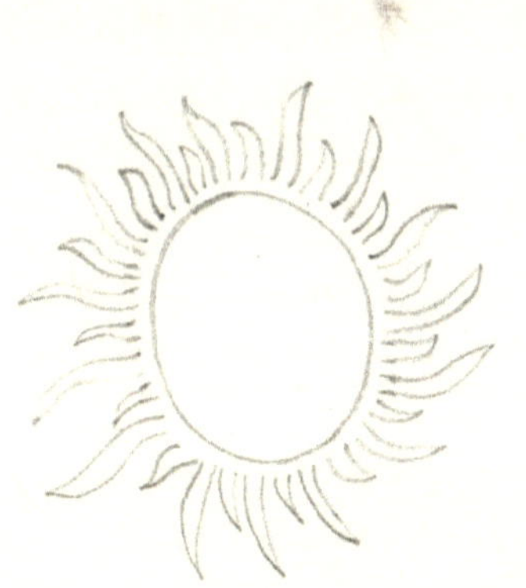

Proud

I have done myself proud.
I can finally say that out loud.
Made myself a little vow.
To be the best somehow.

Under the stars

Here we are, under the stars.

Discovering scars.

Watching mars.

The world is ours.

Happy with my skin

I'm happy with my skin.
I adore my little chin.
For it is a sin.
To not love your skin.

Faith

I have faith.
In the things I create.
I'm doing great.
Blocking the hate.

Just want to be free

You confuse me.
Why don't you see?
I want to be free.
So please let me be.

Beautiful

Our bodies are beautiful.
Then why are we so doubtful?
The fact that some of us don't love our bodies is painful.
It is simply sinful.

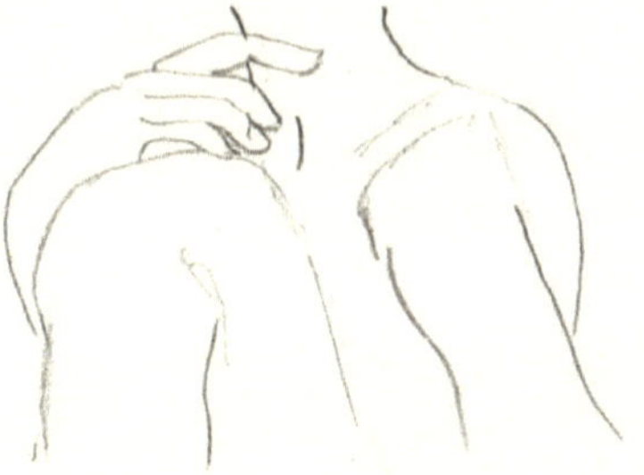

Sunset

Can we stay and watch the sunset?
I really want to forget.
The feeling of regret.
So I can move ahead.

Happier

I'm happier.
You were just a little error.
I'm doing better.
Talking to you was just a blunder.

Believe

Believe in yourself.

Stop putting your feelings on shelf.

Know what to do with yourself.

Yearn for your future self.

A ray

I'm doing okay.
Keeping the negativity at bay.
I'm going to find my way.
I know there's always a ray.

In the moment

Blue skies

Brown eyes

Cold brewed coffee

Smelled like toffee

Fresh air

Don't care

Here I am

Living in the moment not in the past or future.

Loving myself every step

Every moment

Starting now.

Best feeling in the world

The sun hits my face
I finally slow down my pace
Looking up at the sky
Wondering if I could fly
It feels warm
Standing here
In my best form
One I promise to love forever
As I get my feelings together
In this moment
Everything is simply blissful
It's the best feeling in the world.

Love myself

Is it really that wrong to love yourself?
To love every part of you
The good and bad?
Is it really impossible?
Truth is that it's not
It's actually very easy
God made us this for a reason
It's our purpose to fulfill it
To love it no matter what
Anyone says
They probably don't know what they're saying
So please just love yourself
Because you're beautiful.

Greater

You'll always be a hater.
I'm just getting greater.
Wish you could do better.
Well it's not my fault you chose to be bitter.

Gold

I've learned our bodies are gold.

There's so much pain we hold.

We try to be bold.

We do what we're told.

Yet people are always so cold.

Pablo

My dog makes me laugh
He's the best thing I'll ever have
I don't know what I'd do without him
My life would just be so dim
He is one of my reasons to be happier
He is my reason to do better

What matters more

What matter more?
the inside or the outside?
In the world,
The size of our thigh gap matters more
Than the size of our brains
Why do people criticise
us about our size?
Why can we promote body positivity?
There is just too much negativity.
Why can't people be progressive?
Instead of just being so offensive?

Ease

Feeling at peace

I take a step toward

At an ease

I forget about your word

I'm free

Away from the world

I can be me

The sun slowly hitting my face

I find my pace.

Learned to love myself

You never believed me

Never showed me an ounce of love

Even when I always kept you above

When you finally did

It was too late

Because I learned to block your hate

Okay to cry

It's okay to cry
It hurts more to hold it in
It does not make you weak
I know it hurts more to speak
Tears are not meant to be bottled up
They aren't beverages
And if it is not okay to cry
Then why is it okay to lie?

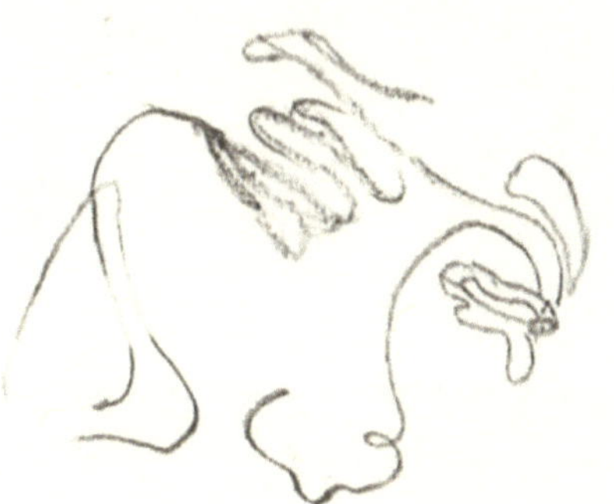

Exquisite

Thank you for calling me exquisite
Even though I really don't deserve it
You really got me through it
And I don't know how to thank you for it.

Dove

It was like a moth to a flame
This time was not the same
It was a direct aim
It was my claim
And suddenly the world seemed less dim.

Happy with being alone

It was the first time where I felt at peace

It was my day to seize

I owed to myself

To be away from the world

Away from people like you

Memories

I'll always cherish those memories
One day I'll let go of the diaries
I can't believe we went from believing in fairies
To believing in enemies.
I guess that's the hard part about growing up
You learn to give up.

Cope

I looked up
With nothing but hope
They finally learned to cope
And he learned to not to mope
It didn't do him any good
I saw it from where I stood
He finally understood.

My best friend

How do you have the energy?
To put up with me
I don't know if I'll ever be as strong as you
I don't think if I can ever manage without you
We may fight
But you'll always be my light.

www.ingramcontent.com/pod-product-compliance
Lightning Source LLC
Chambersburg PA
CBHW061440160726

47995CB00003B/969